22 MAY

D1685969

Primary literacy

WITHDRAWN

First published in 2008 by the Institute of Education, University of London,
20 Bedford Way, London WC1H 0AL
www.ioe.ac.uk/publications

© 2008 Institute of Education, University of London

British Library Cataloguing in Publication Data:
A catalogue record for this publication is available from the British Library

ISBN 978 0 85473 795 6

Design by Andrew Chapman
Typeset by Keystroke, 28 High Street, Tettenhall, Wolverhampton
Printed by DSI Colourworks

Institute of Education • University of London

Primary literacy

Research and practice

Roger Beard

Professor of Primary Education

Based on an inaugural lecture delivered at the Institute of Education,
University of London, on 22 January 2008

Professor Roger Beard

Primary literacy: research and practice

My topic is primary literacy. The focus is on the practice of teaching reading and writing in the primary school age range – 5 to 11 – and its associated professional discourse. I shall use a critical review of some recent developments in the United Kingdom to explore the capacities that research can have in enhancing professionalism.

Deceptively simple words?

The deceptively simple words 'primary' and 'literacy' need a little additional comment. 'Primary' refers to a stage of education largely characterised by generalist teaching, in which one teacher has responsibility for teaching most subjects to a class of children for at least a year. This is largely true not only of England, but also of many other countries.

In England, 'primary' covers six years of children's lives and two stages of statutory curriculum content. It is important to keep the whole of the primary age range in mind in what follows, because some influential studies, although they have 'primary' in the title, have only investigated part of this age range and may have had a disproportionate influence on discussions about the primary phase as a whole.

Similarly, the word 'literacy' has increasingly been used in ways other than its original connotation: the ability to read and write. One recent development has been the use of the term to refer to general competence – as in computer, financial, and even emotional, literacy. This lecture concentrates on what goes on in schools and on the ability to read and write, including some aspects of how this ability may be developed on screen, as well as on paper.

Reading and writing are often justifiably referred to as central parts of 'the basics', but more accurately they may benefit from being recognised as the 'tools of further learning' (Barber, 1997: 174). Children are constrained in accessing their entitlement to the wider curriculum unless they are skilled in utilising the written word.

In contrast, I shall take a more pluralist line on what is meant by 'research', broadly in line with the principles of rigour, originality and significance that inform thinking in the research community. I shall refer to empirical studies with a range of methodologies, research syntheses and scholarly analyses.

Enhancing professionalism through asking fundamental questions

Inevitably, certain values underpin the adoption of any methodology or the scope of any research synthesis. My own value position is that teacher professionalism will be enhanced if fundamental questions about reading and writing are asked that only research can begin to answer (e.g. Beard, 1984, 1987, 1993, 1995a, 2000c, 2005; Oakhill and Beard, 1999; Beard *et al.*, 2008): What are the forms and functions of the language on which literacy builds? What is known about real-world demands on the ability to read and write? What are the significant early aspects of early literacy? How might development be conceptualised and investigated? What kinds of curriculum provisions and teaching practices may be more effective than others in particular contexts, and what kinds of early interventions are effective for children who do not make expected progress?

Literacy 'development'

Perhaps the most notable change in the field for me over the past thirty years or so has been in the area that my PhD addressed: reading *development* (Beard, 1982, 1989; Beard and Thomas, 1985). Knowledge about the skills and strategies needed in the information age has grown and, with the advent of electronic texts, new questions need to be asked about the nature of these texts and the skills that they require (Beard, 2003a). According to David Reinking (1998: xxiv), hypertext has become the quintessential example of how printed and electronic texts differ. The former is generally linear and hierarchical; the latter is fluid – a set of different potential texts awaiting realisation. Hypertext's elements are verbal or graphic units and the links that join them. Hypertexts are multi-linear, constructed so that the textual elements can be read in any order (Bolter, 1991). Such distinctions suggest that the key skills in reading hypertext will need to be underpinned by an understanding of the availability of different routes through the material.

Nevertheless, it is salutary to note that explorations of these issues are still largely located in printed texts, often with little visual supporting material. This apparently confirms Gunther Kress's view that, although 'language-as-writing will increasingly be displaced by image in many domains of public communication . . . writing will remain the preferred mode of the political and cultural elites' (Kress, 2003: 1).

The value of interdisciplinary enquiry

My doctoral work also revealed how the kinds of questions I raised above open up complexities that may be most productively tackled by drawing upon the widest research base that is operationally feasible. I have become increasingly convinced of the value of interdisciplinary enquiry into complex educational issues, whose challenges often stretch far beyond the conceptual reach of a single discipline. While working primarily in applied disciplines, I have also collaborated with others in exploring how far assumptions about how we

3

read and write are commensurate with findings from the relevant basic research literature.

I have also come increasingly to recognise that large-scale application of research findings to practice often brings about the unexpected. Any research-based implementation is likely to benefit from taking account of local factors, sometimes including commercial pressures and the agendas of those who seek to shape public opinion.

At the same time, as Martyn Hammersley has warned, it is important not to raise expectations about what research can and cannot do in meeting practitioner needs (Hammersley, 2002). Indeed part of the challenge in strengthening research–practice links is to encourage frank acceptance of the limitations of research, while also exploring the value of systematic and critical enquiry (Bassey, 1995: 139).

In primary literacy, synthesising findings from research to inform practice has been further constrained by it being characterised by high-profile issues and debates. Furthermore, research and publication in primary education and literacy education have not always been as interconnected as might have been expected.

The changing policy context

In the area of primary literacy, a number of issues have continued to feature in press headlines. The following may sound familiar:

> We are faced with the fact that reading standards today are no better than they were a decade ago . . . there is a high probability that the reading comprehension standards [of 7- to 11-year-olds] have declined somewhat.
>
> (Start and Wells, 1972: 72, 67)

> there is a sizeable minority of both sexes who do not read books in their leisure time. This minority . . . increases with age and reaches at 14+ the disturbingly high proportion of . . . 40 per cent of boys.
>
> (Whitehead *et al.*, 1975: 47)

It might be assumed that such conclusions from major studies would have rallied concerted action in the ensuing years. Yet primary literacy has remained a heavily 'contested' area. It has sometimes been characterised by polarised debates, cult ideas that have been shown to be in some ways misleading, and relatively little 'giving of ground' by proponents of sharply contrasting viewpoints. The substantial changing of views by influential writers in the light of new evidence seems to occur only occasionally in this field (see Stanovich, 1994, for a personal account of the kinds of consequences that can follow).

Perhaps, in part, because of the polarised debates, primary literacy in the UK has also been increasingly influenced by government policy, through the centralising initiatives of the past twenty years or so. The centralisation followed a period when there was little direct central guidance on the curriculum. British primary education has had a long tradition of teacher autonomy in deciding the content of the curriculum, assessment arrangements and teaching methods used. In 1976, the primary school curriculum was described by the Prime Minister, James Callaghan, in a speech at Ruskin College, Oxford, as a 'secret garden'. This was a phrase that reflected the fact that central government had relatively little say in what was taught or the teaching methods that were used.

The Prime Minister's words were to trigger a series of central government reports and reforms that may have gone beyond his expectations (Maclure, 1988; Phillips and Furlong, 2001). Each strand of centralisation has made a distinctive contribution to the critical mass of central policy. Each has brought the potential to undermine or distort the impact of one or more of the others: a statutory national curriculum from 1989 (revised in 1994); statutory national testing at 7 and 11 from 1991 onwards;[1] statutory inspections of schools from 1992 onwards;[2] and non-statutory guidance on how to teach, through a National Literacy Strategy (NLS) (1998 onwards). Each of these four strands of centralisation has evolved from different organisations – all of which have different degrees of delegated powers – and have together added new mediating variables to research–practice relationships.

Teachers have also had to adjust to a range of new demands on their professional roles, adding new dimensions of curriculum delivery, accountability and 'visibility' through publicly available inspection reports. However, it is important to note that such changes, leading to greater professional consistency through standards, codes of practice and increased transparency of procedures, are now common in many countries.

The broader international context

In an International Review of Curriculum and Assessment (INCA) report (Le Métais, 2003) on primary education in twenty countries, it was noted that there is a strong trend towards frequent and wide-ranging reform, covering the governance, management, organisation, content and assessment of learning.

In sixteen countries, responsibility for institutional control now lies with school-level boards, comprising a range of stakeholders. This (relative) autonomy is accompanied in most countries in the study by formal accountability mechanisms such as the publication of schools' aims and activities, as well as outcomes of pupil examinations and school inspections (where conducted).

All twenty countries, except Scotland, have a statutory curriculum, prescribed by national or sub-national authorities. In countries with a tradition of centrally determined curricula, there is a strong trend towards increasing local flexibility within prescribed time allocations.

In all these countries, teachers routinely assess and report on their pupils' progress. There has been a trend towards external assessment – both statutory and voluntary – during the primary phase. This is intended to help teachers identify pupil progress, to plan their work and/or to be an element of school accountability. Five of the countries limit external assessment to sample populations. There is a tendency to publish results, either by school (England and the USA) or as anonymous trends (France, New Zealand and Spain).

There is a trend towards formulating curricula in terms of learning outcomes, but only in a few cases – Australia, Canada (Ontario) and England – are these linked to achievement targets, which specify the percentage of pupils who are expected to achieve a given level.

There is also an increasing tendency to refer to performance in international surveys to explain or justify national policy changes. In some cases, dissatisfaction with performance in international surveys has led to specific programmes.

A national curriculum

The first centralising strand was the introduction of a national curriculum in all four UK countries in 1989, although the actual content varied from country to country. The need for a national curriculum had been indicated in a part-response to Prime Minister Callaghan's words, a representative survey of schools in the 7–11 age range by Her Majesty's Inspectorate, *Primary Education in England* (DES, 1978). The findings highlighted substantial (and long-standing) inconsistencies in curriculum provision between schools. Colin Richards (1982) subsequently pointed out the tension between the inconsistency that results from 'laissez-faire' curriculum provision and a publicly funded comprehensive system of education.

It might seem axiomatic that the introduction of a national curriculum would provide a vehicle for showcasing research–practice links. Yet some of the decisions of the body delegated to oversee the National Curriculum, then called the National Curriculum Council, seemed very questionable in this respect. The original curriculum proved to be overcrowded and had soon to be slimmed down (Dearing, 1994; see also Beard, 1999b) but it also appeared far less informed by *psychological* research than might have been expected (Beard, 1995b). An example was the accumulated research on phonics, the teaching method that helps children to build their understanding of phoneme–grapheme correspondences of written English. In the forty-three pages of the 1989 National Curriculum for English for primary schools, there was only one mention of phonics (DES, 1989: 7). In this instance, it seems to me that research findings have subsequently been used in a 'restorative' capacity in professional discourse and to dignify certain aspects of literacy education practice.[3]

The meagre reference may also have reflected the theories that downplayed the significance of the phonic aspects of reading, which became influential in England in the late 1980s. These theories were described as an 'orthodoxy' in an analysis of initial teacher training booklists for reading courses carried out by the National Foundation for Educational Research (Gorman, 1989; Brooks *et al.*, 1992). Such assumptions flew in the face of a major research synthesis on early reading that was commissioned by the USA Congress at the time (Adams, 1990). The synthesis provided substantial evidence of the importance and complexity of phonics in the teaching and learning of reading and comprised a discussion of peer-reviewed publications, whose list numbered over thirty-five pages. Adams concluded that, when systematic code instruction is included along with the reading and writing of meaningful text, there is superior reading achievement overall, both for 'low-readiness' and better prepared pupils (see also Adams, 1991).

The radical nature of the theories underlying the orthodoxy led to a protracted debate in the UK (e.g. Waterland, 1985; Donaldson, 1989; HMI, 1991; Beard and Oakhill 1994; see also Beard and McKay, 1998) and led to an edited book (Beard, 1993) that explored the notion of balance across linguistic, psychological and literary perspectives. The National Curriculum was revised for implementation in 1995. In the revised version, 'key skills' for reading were spelled out in far greater detail. However, even then, there was still no mention of phonemes (on which the English writing system is primarily based: Venezky, 1970; Carney, 1994), an omission not rectified until further minor amendments in 1999 (Department for Education and Employment, 1999). This raises the issue of how securely the primary teachers were placed to implement the 1998 guidance material that included specific reference to phonemes (Beard and Willcocks, 2002).

Changing notions of 'good practice'

The *teaching* of reading and writing has not always received the attention that might have been expected in primary literacy, particularly the teaching of groups or whole classes. For a large part of my career, 'good practice' in English primary schools has been associated with individualised approaches, sometimes where classes of children tackled several different subject areas at the same time in various kinds of 'integrated day'. One explanation for this may lie in the work of a government commission chaired by Lady Plowden in 1967, whose report (titled *Children and **their** Primary Schools*, my emphasis) seemed to conceptualise good practice by projecting the informality and the more child-centred curriculum provision of early years education upwards into older age ranges (CACE, 1967). It was a report that received searching criticism from senior academics at the Institute of Education (Peters, 1969). In particular, the then Director of the Institute, Lionel Elvin, argued that the report 'gravely underestimated the positive role of the teacher' (Peters, 1969: 85).

It is also a little chastening to note that, of the 495 pages of the Plowden Report, only six were devoted to reading. When, five years later, the NFER report by Start and Wells, quoted above, was published, the UK education system seemed to lack a conceptual and empirical infrastructure to deal with the issues raised, necessitating another committee of inquiry, this time chaired by Sir Alan (later Lord) Bullock. The report, *A Language for Life,* devoted 559 pages to inquiring into 'all aspects of teaching the use of English, including reading, writing and speech'. It took a cautious line on teaching methods, with its much-cited statement that there is no one method, medium, approach, device or philosophy that holds the key to learning to read (DES, 1975: 521).

Yet, when I undertook a review of research and professional publications for my book *Developing Reading 3–13* (Beard, 1987), it was evident that hearing individual children read books from commercially produced reading schemes was widespread. Much professional energy was going into the choice of teaching materials, assessment of progress, record-keeping and meeting special needs, but references to class or group teaching approaches were relatively rare. This conclusion was borne out by subsequent studies by the NFER (Cato *et al.*, 1992); at the University of Warwick (Raban *et al.*, 1993); at the IOE (Ireson *et al.*,1995); and the University of Exeter (Wragg *et al.*, 1998).[4]

This is not to condemn individual teaching methods, which can be highly productive when used in a dedicated way, especially with the 'hardest to teach' children (Clay, 1993; see also Brooks, 2002). However, research was accumulating to indicate that, used as a principal teaching approach in a class of thirty children, individualised approaches often result in fragmented interactions and leave little time for strategic teaching *per se*. Furthermore, evidence reported by Harrison (1999), in a review of reading research in the UK, is that when teachers concentrate their teaching on hearing individual children read, other children in the class may spend up to a third of their time off task.

The 1970s and 1980s saw the publication of reports which questioned the effectiveness and practicality of individualised teaching approaches (e.g. Bennett *et al.*, 1976; Galton *et al.*, 1980), albeit again by investigating the 7–11 age range. The continuing debate about primary practices was reflected in a central government discussion paper (Alexander *et al.*, 1992; see also Hammersley and Scarth, 1992; Galton, 1995) following on from an evaluation of primary education in a northern local education authority (Alexander, 1991).

One of the most influential research studies of the time, which foregrounded the issue of effectiveness, came from the research of another Director of the IOE (Mortimore *et al.*, 1988), *School Matters*, a three-year study of fifty schools (again in the 7–11 age range) emphasised the importance of maximum communication between teachers and pupils, including some whole-class teaching which, in the research study, increased the overall number of contacts with pupils and led to more frequent higher-order communications.[5]

Mortimore's work may be seen as an example of the 'indicative' capacity of research. This is not so much in relation to specific teaching approaches in literacy as to some of the key characteristics that they might reflect – and the classroom conditions in which they may be put into practice. *School Matters* has been seen as making a significant contribution to international research into what makes schools effective and in drawing out implications for school improvement and management (Scheerens, 1992; Reynolds *et al.*, 1994; Creemers, 1994; Teddlie and Reynolds, 1999).

School effectiveness is gauged by the further progress that pupils make – beyond what might be expected from consideration of the school's intake (Mortimore, 1991).[6] School effectiveness findings, and the meta-analyses that are often used, provide a sense of *direction* for school improvement, especially in the light of a core of findings from a variety of studies in several different countries (see Davies, 2000; Goldstein and Woodhouse, 2000; and Reynolds and Teddlie, 2001, for a discussion of some recurrent issues).

Using research to influence practice: the NLS

In a paper in the *Oxford Review of Education* in 2000 (Beard, 2000a) I outlined how research into school and teacher effectiveness seemed to me to be one of the 'predisposing' influences that shaped the nature and structure of the National Literacy Strategy (NLS) in England. The NLS was the fourth centralising initiative referred to earlier, although it lacked the statutory status of the other three. The *ORE* paper was based on an independent review of the research and other related evidence that I had been commissioned to write (Beard, 1999a). My review reported that, over the previous thirty years, standards in literacy in England had apparently not increased in line with the hopes and expectations of policymakers. The largely individualised teaching of early literacy appeared to be out of line with the practices suggested by school effectiveness research.

The need to target standards had been given priority in the light of research findings from comparisons of reading attainment in different countries (Elley 1992; Brooks *et al.*, 1996). The research had indicated that England and Wales was located within a 'middle' group of countries. In the middle and upper parts of the range of scores, children in England and Wales performed as well as those in countries much higher in the rank order. However, a distinctive feature of UK performance was the existence of a long 'tail' of underachievement which was proportionately greater than that of other countries.

This underachievement seemed to call for the kinds of direct interactive teaching approaches which had been successful with 'at risk' pupils in the USA and Australia (e.g. Slavin, 1997; Crevola and Hill, 1998). These included greater use of whole-class approaches (such as shared reading and writing) and group approaches (guided reading and writing) whose potential for more extensive use in the UK had already been noted in London by the Centre for Language in Primary Education (CLPE, 1990).

The 'precipitating' influence seemed to me to be the early success of the National Literacy Project (NLP). This had been set up by the previous government in its final year of office in 1996 in a sample of English local education authorities. Its aims included improving standards of literacy in participating primary schools in line with national expectations and providing support to schools and teachers through a structured programme and consultancy support. This support included a *Framework for Teaching,* which translated the National Curriculum (DfE, 1995) into termly objectives, and a daily 'literacy hour'. The NLP was led by a senior member of Her Majesty's Inspectorate, John Stannard, who saw the Framework as providing schools with a means of shifting the emphasis in planning for the revised National Curriculum for English from 'what' to 'how', presenting teachers with a wide range of new decisions about tasks, activities and methods (Stannard, 1997; Stannard and Huxford, 2007).

The NLP was independently evaluated by the National Foundation for Educational Research, using data from 250 schools. It may be seen as an example of the 'evaluative' capacity of research, effectively a pilot study of an ambitious curriculum-reform programme. The test results revealed a significant and substantial improvement over the eighteen-month period, using a range of independent tests. Children eligible for free school meals, those with special educational needs and those learning English as an additional language had lower scores, but all these groups also made statistically significant progress. All ethnic groups benefited equally (Sainsbury *et al.,* 1998).

While the evaluation findings from the NLP were impressive, caveats need to be added: the schools where the NLP was implemented were generally in disadvantaged areas where there were arguably greater possibilities for improvement in educational attainment. In addition, the data on writing were far more limited and less holistic than the data on reading, being largely limited to accuracy.

The NLS was the result of the work of a Literacy Task Force (1997a) that had been set up by the then Shadow Secretary of State for Education and Employment, David Blunkett, in May 1996.[7] The Literacy Task Force recommendation was that every primary school should adopt the Framework unless it could demonstrate through its action plan, schemes of work and test performances that its own approach was at least as effective as that of the use of the literacy hour (Literacy Task Force, 1997b). In my view, the challenge that this recommendation represented has not resulted in the publication of the research-based alternatives that might have been expected. As I in part antici-pated in another paper at that time (Beard, 2000b), where alternative emphases have been mooted, they have largely concerned the timing and emphasis of the phonics elements of the strategy (e.g. McGuinness 1998; Watson and Johnson 1998) which have in turn led to the Rose Review (Rose, 2006).

The NLS appears to have increased pupil attainment in primary school children, as measured in the results from the national tests that are annually administered to 11-year-olds, although the significance of this trend remains disputed. The NLS,[8] together with the companion National Numeracy Strategy (NNS), has been described by a world authority on educational change as the most ambitious large-scale strategy of educational reform witnessed since the 1960s (Fullan, 2000: 1). As such, it can provide insights into the complex relationships between research, policy and practice. These relationships were evident in the evaluation of the NLS/NNS by the Ontario Institute for Studies in Education (Earl *et al.*, 2003). These evaluative studies, because of their con-ceptual range, seem to me also to illustrate the 'generative' capacity of research, opening up new issues for investigation, some of which were unforeseen at the outset.

The final Ontario report identifies the successes of the NLS/NNS as: the breadth of influence on teaching and learning; its adaptation within a coherent vision; value for money; policy coherence over time; and the balance of 'pres-sure and support'. The evaluation also raises issues about how a strategy can be sustained through adaptation and ownership in schools while maintaining adherence to the key teaching and learning principles that are involved. It iden-tifies the need to develop greater 'assessment literacy' in schools – the use of assessment data for formative purposes in specifying and critically analysing what children need to learn next (rather than just in recording what children have achieved). It discusses the importance of extending the strategy to parents, families and the public.

The evaluation also raises several other issues: programme fidelity; the role of subject knowledge in professional development; and the unanticipated con-sequences of implementation.[9]

The national evaluation of *Further Literacy Support*

Some of these issues came to the fore in a national evaluation of a later strand of the NLS, *Further Literacy Support* (FLS) led by a team directed by Professor Diane Shorrocks-Taylor and myself at the University of Leeds. The 'adaptation of the NLS within a coherent vision' led to extra resources being devoted to issues identified in implementation. These included supplemental, 'layered' assistance for pupils aged 5–6, 7–8 and 9–10 who need additional support in literacy learning. FLS was introduced in 2003 and is an intervention programme to assist 9- to 10-year-olds whose projected attainment at 11 may place them at risk in accessing the secondary school curriculum. It comprises twelve weeks of additional support in Term 2 (spring) for approximately 20% of an average class (about six children). The children are taught in withdrawal groups by a teaching assistant, using scripted materials.

The effectiveness of this programme was investigated through an externally commissioned, independent national evaluation study, using standardised tests and teacher assessments of a national sample of over 1200 children (Beard *et al.*, 2004). Test scores and teacher assessments from the national evaluation of FLS indicated short-term catch-up in reading by the target group and subsequent sustained movement similar to other 9- to 10-year-old pupils over two terms. Similar, but not statistically significant, catch-up was found in writing. There was some evidence of further catch-up by the target group between Year 5 and Year 6, but this was not significant.

Case studies of twenty schools indicated that schools where children made higher progress had implemented the programme with high degrees of fidelity and with regular links being made between the work of the FLS group and that of the rest of the class. The skill and tenacity of teaching assistants were very apparent, often in the face of challenging new extensions to their role. Regular discussions between teachers and teaching assistants were also very evident in these schools, although the professional experience of the teachers and teaching assistants was sometimes relatively limited.

National test data, from a year after the programme ended, indicate that over 90% of the target children did meet or exceed 'national expectations' in reading at age 11, and 84% did in English overall. As bringing children up to age-related attainment at age 11 is the primary purpose of the FLS programme, these data are an important measure of its success.

One of the most interesting issues that the FLS study opens up is that little research seems to have been done on the effectiveness of supplemental programmes for the 9–10 age range (McIntyre *et al.*, 2005). Early and individual interventions are generally seen as more effective. The FLS evaluation indicated that later, group intervention can also be effective and that its outcomes can be sustained. The study also provides some evidence of the effectiveness of classroom assistants at delivering intervention programmes of an appropriate model (albeit a heavily scripted one) and gives insights into the training investment potential of para-professionals.

The issue of writing

In a paper in the *Journal of Research in Reading* (Beard, 2000b) in 2000, I noted that the NLS Framework also included guidance on the continuation of three practices that pre-dated the NLS: reading to the class (e.g. in end-of-day sessions), promoting pupils' own independent reading (for interest and pleasure) and extended writing. I have written imploringly about these recommendations in the professional literature (e.g. Beard, 2002, 2003b) and there is only space here for discussion of the third of these – extended writing.

In the *JRR* paper, I warned that, in relation to extended writing, much would depend on teachers' skill in linking their literacy-hour teaching and learning to the curriculum contexts of writing in other subject areas. The practice of setting pupils in attainment groups for the literacy hour might constrain these links unless communications between teachers were consciously increased. I further warned that the full potential of guided writing might not be widely understood.

By coincidence, the teaching of writing became an issue of concern that year when Her Majesty's Inspectorate (2000) published a discussion paper highlighting 'underachievement' in writing, as shown by national test results, compared with reading, especially among boys. The paper was significantly titled *The Teaching of Writing in Primary Schools: Could Do Better.*

HMI (2000) suggest that a number of factors may have contributed to the underachievement, including: the legacy of reliance on decontextualised exercises; insufficient teaching of writing; pupils practising writing rather than being taught how to improve it; a lack of balance between the teaching of writing and reading; and insufficient transfer of literacy learning into other subjects.

This state of affairs may also illustrate the restorative capacity potential of research. Current practice may be insufficiently influenced by research findings on: the importance of content knowledge, as well as discourse knowledge; the importance of purpose and audience, as well as form and structure; and the potential role of various facilitative procedures that support the composing of writing (Bereiter and Scardamalia, 1987; Beard, 1984, 1991, 2000c, 2005; see also Peacock and Beard, 1997). However, a more wide-ranging review of research and practice also seemed necessary.

Reconceptualising Writing 5–16

In part response to the HMI report, in 2003, I collaborated with Debra Myhill at the University of Exeter and Jeni Riley at the Institute of Education to address these issues by securing funding from the Economic and Social Research Council for an international seminar series.[10] The seminars allowed an examination of the issues and challenges that writing presents for pupils from several disciplines and across the 5–16 age range. The papers and discussion transcripts may be found at http://www.ioe.ac.uk/schools/ecpe/ReconceptualisingWriting 5-16/index.html.

In addressing current concerns, there are timely reminders and caveats in the seminar paper by George Hillocks (2003) who reports on the findings from a meta-analysis of research on the teaching of writing that began with examining nearly 500 studies (also see Hillocks, 1986, 1995). In the original analysis, seventy-three had research designs that were judged to meet the criteria for good research. The study distinguishes between the mode and focus of instruction.

The modes examined included the presentational, individualised, natural process, and environmental teaching.[11]

Teachers may, of course, use a judicious mix of the four approaches. Given the current drive to raise standards in English schools, there may be an understandable gravitation towards a presentational approach, when this is closest to the mode used in the national test assessments. But it is towards the potential of the environmental mode (approximating to what is now called 'guided writing' in the UK) that Hillocks steers us. This mode was significantly more effective than the natural process approach and substantially more effective than the presentational approach. Teachers in this mode, in contrast to the presentational, tend to minimise lecture, recitation, and silent individual seat work. Rather they focus on developing activities that lead from scaffolded work under the teacher's direction, to small-group work, to independent work on the same kind of task. The activities they invent are aimed at learning whatever strategies are necessary to the writing prior to undertaking it.

Hillocks also asks us to consider the focus of instruction. This has to do with the teaching of various kinds of grammar, and providing and discussing models of particular kinds of writing – sentence combining, learning scales for judging writing, free writing, and inquiry.[12] Inquiry (engagement with the subject matter) has many dimensions, beginning with careful observation and representation in language of the phenomena observed, questioning at every stage, comparing and contrasting of the phenomena observed to develop interpretations, imagining relationships leading to tentative hypotheses and theories, testing of tentative hypotheses through formal tests based on some rule of evidence, evaluating the tests and the evidence for conclusions, and developing theories that have predictive value. He reports that not all of these dimensions have been examined in relationship to composition, but those that have show greater power than anything else in the research. It seems to me that, in restoring balance to this area of the primary curriculum, it is the *content* of the primary curriculum that may hold a valuable key.

New enquiries into writing development

The ESRC seminars have subsequently formed the embryo of an international handbook (Beard *et al.*, 2008) with thirty-eight chapters from over a dozen countries. The title of the handbook – *Handbook of Writing Development* – indicates that the seminars raised a range of questions about, among other things, what comprises development in writing and how it is conceptualised.

In a recently completed research project (Beard *et al.*, 2007) I have responded to some of these questions by investigating the development in narrative and persuasive writing in a sample of 112 primary school children over a twelve-month period, using a repeat-design and a range of textual and syntactical criteria. The study indicated that, while there were some developments in features of sentence grammar and technical accuracy, a more consistent and positive range of results was found through the use of new genre-specific scales. The study revealed unexpected subtleties in how writing develops across genres and between genders.[13]

Conclusion

Research in education has been the subject of extensive debate since the paper by David Hargreaves (1996) over a decade ago. I have tried to show how research has a number of capacities to enhance professionalism by lifting teaching and professional discourse above custom and practice and the potential inconsistencies of localised agendas.

I have reiterated the value of interdisciplinary enquiry into complex educational issues and of recognising the importance of extending the research–practice focus to allow for the 'law of unexpected outcomes'. A case in point is the current roll-out of the Rose Review – the discrete teaching of synthetic phonics – into school contexts. This provides new opportunities for investigating, in teachers, the use of a body of knowledge that has only recently been accumulated for pedagogical purposes, and, in children, the attention to aspects of language and literacy that may differ from the aspects of emergent literacy developed in their preschool years. In some respects, in this area of primary literacy, the research–practice dialogue has only just begun.

In a recent paper the current Director of the Institute of Education has referred to Michael Barber's view that we may be moving now from a period of 'informed prescription' in the UK to a post-centralisation period of 'informed professionalism'. This is seen as a new phase, just beginning, when teachers will have appropriate knowledge, skills and attitudes, so that the government can grant them a greater degree of licensed autonomy to manage their own affairs (Whitty, 2006: 2).

There appears to be widespread agreement that, in primary literacy, the profile of subject knowledge has been raised in recent years. In this instance, the many centralising reforms in the UK have appeared to complement, rather than distort, the influences of each other. Similarly, the skills of teaching have been foregrounded, and pedagogy has now taken central place in professional discourse. The most productive permutations of class, group and individual approaches are subjected to unprecedented critical scrutiny. While professional attitudes to primary literacy may be less well-researched, the National Year of Reading, fronted by the National Literacy Trust in 2008, is likely to promote new interest in this area.

Such aspects of 'informed professionalism' can provide opportunities for future participation in globalised dialogues that are being prompted by the international trends in curricula, assessment, accountability and performance surveys referred to earlier. This lecture has shown that sustained attention to the outcomes from scholarship and systematic and critical enquiry has much to offer this future, in primary literacy in particular – and in education as a whole.

Notes

1   The second centralising initiative was an annual programme of national testing for 7-, 11- and 14-year-old pupils that began in 1991. Again, arrangements varied among the four countries and assumed a higher profile in England because of the publication of league tables based on the performances of individual schools. The assessment system was originally based on discrete groups of specific criteria, which were equated to different levels of attainment, from

Level 1 (the lowest) to Level 8, in a rather formulaic way. Following the revision of the National Curriculum in 1994–95, however, broad 'level descriptions' have been used, on a 'best fit' basis.

There has also been a more subtle – some would say insidious – change. When the tests were first developed, the modal attainment for 11-year-olds was Level 4. Since then, the government body delegated to oversee curriculum and assessment has equated Level 4 with the notion of 'national expectation', as a part of a broader target-setting culture that central governments of both main political parties have adopted. The high stakes culture created by the testing regime has represented a risk of distorting the teaching and learning potential of the National Curriculum and, when it was eventually introduced, the NLS. For a historical review of national testing in the UK, see Shorrocks-Taylor (1999).

2 The third centralising initiative is that, since 1992, the 19,000 publicly funded English primary schools have also been subjected to a programme of school inspections every four years. The inspections are undertaken by specially trained inspectors, coordinated by the central government's Office for Standards in Education (Ofsted) which was set up in that year. Inspections usually last a week and have normally covered the following: the standards achieved; teaching quality; curricular and extra-curricular activities; student care; partnership with parents; and the school's leadership and management.

Before 1992, schools were inspected by Her Majesty's Inspectorate (HMI), although the small size of the Inspectorate (about 300) meant that individual schools were only fully inspected, on average, once every thirty years or so. The new national database of inspection evidence is now used to produce annual reviews and other subject-specific publications. Meanwhile, the size of HMI has been reduced to about half of what it was. Its new role includes monitoring the training of inspectors and school inspections and undertaking special investigations, for instance a longitudinal evaluation of the National Literacy Strategy (HMI, 2002).

There has again been the potential for the inspection programme, in conjunction with the testing regime, to distort the impact of one or more of the other strands of centralisation. An inspection of an individual school takes account of the school's national test results and draws on data that compare these results with those from schools with similar socio-economic catchments. The inspections can thus inadvertently distort schools' priorities and curriculum provision in ways that may not have been intended when the inspection programme was set up.

Since 2005, the inspection of schools has been relaxed in one way, in that inspections for unproblematic schools are now shorter and more self-evaluative. However, inspections are more pressured in another way, in that schools now have only a few days' (as opposed to several weeks') warning of a forthcoming inspection, and may exist in a state of nervous apprehension.

3 This is not to imply that there was little or no phonics teaching in many schools at that time. In an evaluation of the implementation of the National Curriculum, it was found that, of the

methods of teaching early reading observed by researchers in a sample of schools in a national evaluation, by far the most commonly used approach was pupils reading from a book with a teacher or another adult. Phonics was the second most observed teaching approach, amounting to 16% of observed time, although three-quarters of that time was described as 'self-contained' exercises (Raban *et al.*, 1993).

4 These findings were supported by surveys by Her Majesty's Inspectorate and the Office for Standards in Education. For instance, in 1991 an HMI inspection review reported 'explicit reading instruction, whether to the whole class, groups or individuals, was rarely seen' (HMI, 1991: 16). There was little use of regular direct class or group teaching of reading, even when the design of commercial materials suggested it (Office for Standards in Education, 1996).

5 The report also highlighted the value of the following: structured sessions, involving a teacher-organised framework but allowing pupils to exercise a degree of independence; intellectually challenging teaching, in which teachers used higher-order questions and statements and encouraged pupils to use creative imagination and problem-solving; an attractive, work-centred environment, with a high level of pupil industry and low noise levels and in which teachers spent more time discussing the content of work with pupils and less time on routine matters and work maintenance; limited focus within sessions, in which lessons are organised around one curriculum area (or, at the very most, two) with some differentiation as needed; and the inclusion in lessons of 'audits' of which tasks have been achieved and of what has been learned.

6 Key features of school effectiveness are as follows: the measures used are normally derived from attainment in basic subjects, especially reading, numeracy and examination results; the most valid research is longitudinal, so that one or more cohorts can be followed over time, and a school's consistency and stability can be investigated; and the outcomes from this research are inappropriate for the production of 'blueprint' schools and practices. The analyses used are often correlational, using multi-level statistical techniques; they do not pertain to identify causal relationships. However, the studies provide valuable background and insights for those concerned with school improvement, as there is a core of consistency to be found across a variety of studies in several different countries.

7 The Task Force, led by Professor Michael Barber, then at the Institute of Education, published a preliminary consultation report in February 1997 and a final report in August 1997 (Literacy Task Force, 1997a, 1997b). In its final report the Task Force set out the details of a 'steady, consistent strategy' for raising standards of literacy which could be sustained over a long period of time and be made a central priority for the education service as a whole. The main aspects of the Strategy were as follows:

(a) An initial national target that, by 2002, 80% of 11-year-olds should reach the standard 'expected' for their age in English (National Curriculum Level 4). The proportion reaching this standard in 1996 was 57%. In the event, the target was reached in reading but not in writing. An even more ambitious target of 85% for 2007 replaced it.

(b) A *Framework for Teaching*, an A4-sized ring binder which sets out termly teaching objectives for the 5–11 age range, based on the National Curriculum, and provides a practical structure of time and class management for a daily literacy hour.

(c) A programme of professional development for all primary school teachers, centred on a *Literacy Training Pack*.

8 More recently, the NLS and its companion National Numeracy Strategy have been brought together as part of a broader National Primary Strategy, with encouragement for teachers to maintain a broader curriculum and to give greater attention to creativity, assessment for learning, and health and physical education.

9 Some of these issues are shown on the evaluation of the NLS by Her Majesty's Inspectorate, who surveyed practice in a national sample of 300 schools over a four-year period and provided regular interim reports as well as a final one (HMI, 2002). There had been increases in direct teaching, a clearer structure, higher expectations of pupils and greater progression and continuity. There were also continuing concerns, again reflecting what Reynolds (1998) had prophetically called 'unreliable implementation': the teaching of phonics was insufficiently systematic; guided reading was still not well taught in many schools; day-to-day assessment was not being sufficiently linked to progress; and the NLS was insufficiently embedded in the National Curriculum.

10 We drew together researchers and scholars from relevant disciplines from the UK, the rest of Europe and the USA. The seminars were planned to allow a critical review of the evidence base, to consider the key issues that are raised by the application of different disciplinary perspectives and to explore research and policy issues for the future.

We noted that publications in this field are often age-specific and lack attention to cross-phase implications. Similarly, publications are often limited to a narrow disciplinary perspective, thus delimiting the research–policy interface and constraining the synergetic potential of cross-disciplinary inquiry and discussion.

11 The *presentational* mode is characterised by: (1) relatively clear objectives, e.g. to use particular rhetorical techniques; (2) lecture and teacher-led discussion of the concepts to be learned and applied; (3) the study of models and other materials which explain and illustrate the concept; (4) specific assignments which generally involve following a pattern or following rules that have been previously discussed; and (5) feedback following the writing, coming primarily from teachers.

In the *individualised* mode, students have one-on-one instruction through tutorials or programmed materials that allow students to work at their own rate and teachers to work with individuals.

The *natural process* mode is characterised by: (1) very general objectives, if any are included; (2) free writing about whatever interests the students, often in a journal; (3) writing for audiences of peers with no criteria stipulated; (4) generally positive feedback from peers; (5) opportunities to revise and rework writing; and (6) high levels of interaction among peers. Proponents of this sort of writing instruction usually refer to the teacher as a 'facilitator', whose role is to maintain a positive classroom atmosphere in order to free the imagination and to promote growth in writing, though the growth remains undefined.

The *environmental* mode was so named because, rather than being student-centred or teacher-centred, it is dependent upon the interaction of teachers, students, concepts, and materials. It is characterised by: (1) clear and precise objectives (e.g. to describe a sea shell using figurative language and specific detail); (2) materials and problems selected by the teacher for the purpose of engaging students in specifiable processes important to some particular aspect of writing; (3) activities, such as small peer-group problem-solving discussions conducive to high-level peer interaction related to specific tasks.

12 These six foci of instruction fall into two major categories: form and substance. The studies that focus on grammar, sentence-combining, models and judging writing all deal with aspects of form. Free writing and inquiry deal with the substance of writing. Although free writing directs student attention to the possible subject of their writing, inquiry focuses on teaching strategies by which students can produce the content of their writing.

13 There were significant differences in children's abilities to write in a style appropriate to audience and purpose, select and sequence information in the format of the two genres, construct paragraphs, use a variety of sentences, link ideas and choose words which enhance the writing. In narrative texts, there were significant gains by boys in nine features, and by girls in four; in persuasive texts, there were significant gains by boys in one feature, and by girls in six. Further data analysis showed that there were substantial proportions of children whose writing included a feature in one year but not the other, thus revealing subtle changes within the overall profile.

The analysis also provided evidence of differential development in the two genres between genders. Teachers in the five schools reported being unaware of these relative differences in gender performance and were not able to link them to specific curriculum provision.

References

Adams, M.J. (1990) *Beginning to Read: Thinking and Learning about Print.* Cambridge, MA: MIT Press.

Adams, M.J. (1991) 'Why not Phonics *and* Whole Language?' in W. Ellis (ed.) *All Language and the Creation of Literacy.* Baltimore, MD: Orton Dyslexia Society.

Alexander, R. (1991) *Primary Education in Leeds.* Leeds: University of Leeds.

Alexander, R., Rose, J. and Woodhead, C. (1992) *Curriculum Organisation and Classroom Practice in Primary Schools: A Discussion Paper.* London: Department of Education and Science.

Barber, M. (1997) *The Learning Game: Arguments for an Education Revolution.* London: Indigo.

Bassey, M. (1995) *Creating Education Through Research.* Edinburgh: British Educational Research Association.

Beard, R. (1982) 'Course Evaluation and the Repertory Grid: A humanistic assessment of the influence of an in-service course on teachers and, indirectly, on their pupils'. Unpublished PhD thesis, Brunel University.

Beard, R. (1984) *Children's Writing in the Primary School.* Sevenoaks: Hodder & Stoughton.

Beard, R. (1987) *Developing Reading 3–13.* Sevenoaks: Hodder & Stoughton (Second edition: 1990).

Beard, R. (1989) 'Making Sense of an In-service Reading Course', *British Journal of In-service Education,* 15, 2, 103–109.

Beard, R. (1991) 'Learning to Read like a Writer', *Educational Review,* 43, 1, 17–24.

Beard, R. (ed.) (1993) *Teaching Literacy: Balancing Perspectives.* London: Hodder & Stoughton.

Beard, R. (ed.) (1995a) *Rhyme, Reading and Writing.* London: Hodder & Stoughton.

Beard, R. (1995b) 'Learning to Read: Psychology and Education' in E. Funnell and M. Stuart (eds) *Learning to Read: Psychology in the Classroom.* Oxford: Blackwell.

Beard, R. (1999a) *National Literacy Strategy: Review of Research and other Related Evidence.* London: Department for Education and Employment.

Beard, R. (1999b) 'English: Range, Key Skills and Language Study' in J. Riley and R. Prentice (eds) *The Curriculum for 7–11 Year Olds.* London: Paul Chapman.

Beard, R. (2000a) 'Research and the National Literacy Strategy', *Oxford Review of Education,* 26, 3/4, 421–436.

Beard, R. (2000b) 'Long Overdue? Another Look at the National Literacy Strategy', *Journal of Research in Reading*, 23, 3, 245–255.

Beard, R. (2000c) *Developing Writing 3–13*. London: Hodder & Stoughton.

Beard, R. (2002) Open letter, *English 4–11* (April).

Beard, R. (2003a) 'Uncovering the Key Skills of Reading' in N. Hall, J. Larson and J. Marsh (eds) *Handbook of Early Literacy Research*. London: Sage.

Beard, R. (2003b) 'Breadth, Balance and the Literacy Hour', *Primary History*, 34, 9–11.

Beard, R. (2005) 'Teaching Writing: Using Research to inform Practice' in G. Rijlaarsdam, H. Van den Bergh and M. Couzijn (eds) *Research in Effective Learning and Teaching of Writing*. Amsterdam: Kluwer.

Beard, R. and McKay, M. (1998) 'An Unfortunate Distraction: The real books debate, 10 years on', *Educational Studies*, 24, 1, 69–81.

Beard, R. and Oakhill, J. (1994) *Reading by Apprenticeship? A critique of the Apprenticeship Approach to the Teaching of Reading*. Slough: National Foundation for Educational Research.

Beard, R. and Thomas, L.F. (1985) 'Personal Constructs in the Context of INSET', *British Journal of In-Service Education*, 11, 2, 112–118.

Beard, R. and Willcocks, J. (2002) 'The National Literacy Strategy in England: Changing Phonics Teaching?' in D. Schallert, C.M. Fairbanks, J. Worthy, B. Maloch, and J.V. Hoffman (eds) *51st Yearbook of the National Reading Conference*, pp. 94–105. Wisconsin: National Reading Conference.

Beard, R., Pell, G., Shorrocks-Taylor, D. and Swinnerton, B., with Sawyer, V., Willcocks, J. and Yeomans, D. (2004) *National Evaluation of the National Literacy Strategy Further Literacy Support Programme: Final Report*. London: Department for Education and Skills.

Beard, R., Burrell, A., Pell, G. and Swinnerton, B. (2007) 'Investigating Development in Writing in 9–11 Year Olds' in M. Conrick and M. Howard (eds) *From Applied Linguistics to Linguistics Applied: Issues, Practices, Trends*. Birmingham: British/Irish Association of Applied Linguistics.

Beard. R., Myhill, D., Nystrand, M. and Riley, J. (eds) (2008) *Handbook of Writing Development*. London: Sage.

Bennett, N. with Jordan, J., Long, G. and Wade, B. (1976) *Teaching Styles and Pupil Progress*. London: Open Books.

Bereiter, C. and Scardamalia, M. (1987) *The Psychology of Written Composition*. Hillsdale, NJ: Lawrence Erlbaum.

Bolter, J.D. (1991) *Writing Space: The Computer, Hypertext and the History of Writing.* Hillsdale, NJ: Lawrence Erlbaum.

Brooks, G. (2002) *What Works for Children with Literacy Difficulties? The Effectiveness of Intervention Schemes.* London: Department for Education and Skills.

Brooks, G., Gorman, T., Kendall, L. and Tate, A. (1992*). What Teachers in Training are Taught about Reading.* Slough: National Foundation for Educational Research.

Brooks, G., Pugh, A.K. and Schagen, I. (1996) *Reading Performance at Nine.* Slough: National Foundation for Educational Research.

Carney, E. (1994) *A Survey of English Spelling.* London: Routledge.

Cato, V., Fernandes, C., Gorman, T., Kispal, A. with White, J. (1992) *The Teaching of Initial Literacy: How Do Teachers Do It?* Slough: National Foundation for Educational Research.

Central Advisory Council For Education (1967) *Children and their Primary Schools* (The Plowden Report). London: HMSO.

Centre for Language in Primary Education (1990) *Shared Reading, Shared Writing.* London: Inner London Education Authority/Centre for Language in Primary Education.

Clay, M.M. (1993) *Reading Recovery: A Guidebook for Teachers in Training.* London: Heinemann.

Creemers, B.P.M. (1994) *The Effective Classroom.* London: Cassell.

Crevola, C.A. and Hill, P.W. (1998) 'Evaluation of a Whole-School Approach to Prevention and Intervention in Early Literacy', *Journal of Education for Students Placed At Risk*, 3, 2, 133–157.

Davies, P. (2000) 'The Relevance of Systematic Reviews to Educational Policy and Practice', *Oxford Review of Education,* 26, 365–378.

Dearing, R. (1994) *The National Curriculum and its Assessment: Final Report.* London: School Curriculum and Assessment Authority.

Department for Education (1995) *English in the National Curriculum.* London: HMSO.

Department of Education and Science (1975) *A Language for Life* (The Bullock Report). London: HMSO.

Department of Education and Science (1978) *Primary Education in England.* London: HMSO.

Department of Education and Science (1989) *English for Ages 5 to 11.* London: HMSO.

Department for Education and Employment (1999) *The National Curriculum:*

Handbook for Primary Teachers in England, Key Stages 1 and 2. London: Department for Education and Employment/Qualifications and Curriculum Authority.

Donaldson, M. (1989) *Sense and Sensibility: Some Thoughts on the Teaching of Literacy* (Occasional paper no. 3). Reading: Reading and Language Information Centre, University of Reading. Reprinted in Beard (1993).

Earl, L., Watson, N., Levin, B., Leithwood, K., Fullan, M. and Torrance, N. (2003) *Watching and Learning 3: Final Report of the External Evaluation of England's National Literacy and Numeracy Strategies.* London: Department for Education and Employment.

Elley, W.B. (1992) *How in the World do Students Read?* Hamburg: International Association for the Evaluation of Educational Achievement.

Fullan, M. (2000) 'The Return of Large-scale Reform', *Journal of Educational Change* 1, 5–28.

Galton, M. (1995) *Crisis in the Primary Classroom.* London: David Fulton.

Galton, M., Simon, B. and Croll, P., with Jasman, A. and Willcocks, J. (1980) *Inside the Primary Classroom.* London: Routledge & Kegan Paul.

Goldstein, H. and Woodhouse, G. (2000) 'School Effectiveness Research and Education Policy', *Oxford Review of Education* 26, 353–363.

Gorman, T. (1989). *What Teachers in Training Read about Reading* (Occasional paper no. 4). Slough: National Foundation for Education Research.

Hammersley, M. (2002) *Educational Research: Policymaking and Practice.* London: Paul Chapman.

Hammersley, M. and Scarth, J. (1992) 'Beware of Wise Men Bearing Gifts: A case study in the issue of educational research', *British Educational Research Journal*, 19, 5, 489–498.

Hargreaves, D.H. (1996) *Teaching as a Research-based Profession: Possibilities and Prospects.* London: Teacher Training Agency.

Harrison, C. (1999) 'Reading Research in the United Kingdom' in M.L. Kamil, P.B. Mosenthal, P.D. Pearson and R. Barr (eds) *Handbook of Reading Research.* Hillsdale, NJ: Lawrence Erlbaum.

Her Majesty's Inspectorate (1991) *The Teaching and Learning of Reading in Primary Schools 1990: A Report by HMI.* Stanmore: Department of Education and Science.

Her Majesty's Inspectorate (2000) *The Teaching of Writing in Primary Schools: Could Do Better.* London: Department for Education and Skills.

Her Majesty's Inspectorate (2002) *The National Literacy Strategy: The First Four Years.* London: Office for Standards in Education.

Hillocks, G. (1986) *Research on Written Composition*. Urbana, IL: National Conference on Research in English/ERIC Clearinghouse on Reading and Communication Skills.

Hillocks, G. (1995) *Teaching Writing as Reflective Practice*. New York: Teachers College Press.

Hillocks, G. (2003) *Reconceptualizing Writing Curricula: What We Know and Can Use*. Online. <http://www.ioe.ac.uk/schools/ecpe/ReconceptualisingWriting5-16/docs/hillocks.pdf> (accessed 14 November 2007).

Ireson, J., Blatchford, P. and Joscelyne, T. (1995) 'What Do Teachers Do? Classroom activities in the initial teaching of reading', *Educational Psychology*, 15, 3, 245–256.

Kress, G. (2003) *Literacy in the New Media Age*. London: Routledge.

Le Métais, J. (2003) *International Trends in Primary Education: INCA Thematic Study No. 9*. Online. <http://www.inca.org.uk/pdf/thematic_study_9.pdf > (accessed 14 November 2007).

Literacy Task Force (1997a) *A Reading Revolution: How We Can Teach Every Child to Read Well*. London: Literacy Task Force c/o University of London, Institute of Education.

Literacy Task Force (1997b) *The Implementation of the National Literacy Strategy*. London: Department for Education and Employment.

Maclure, S. (1988) *Education Re-formed*. London: Hodder & Stoughton.

McGuinness, D. (1998) *Why Children Can't Read*. London: Penguin.

McIntyre, E., Jones, D., Powers, S., Newsome, F., Petrosko, J., Powell, R. and Bright, K. (2005). 'Supplemental Instruction in Early Reading: Does it matter for struggling readers?' *The Journal of Educational Research*, 99, 2, 99–107.

Mortimore, P. (1991) 'The Nature and Findings of School Effectiveness Research in the Primary Sector' in S. Riddell and S. Brown (eds) *School Effectiveness Research: Its Messages for School Improvement*. London: HMSO.

Mortimore, P., Sammons, P., Stoll, L., Lewis, D. and Ecob, R. (1988) *School Matters: The Junior Years*. Wells: Open Books.

Oakhill, J. and Beard, R. (eds) (1999) *Reading Development and the Teaching of Reading*. Oxford: Blackwell.

Office for Standards in Education (1996) *The Teaching of Reading in 45 Inner London Primary Schools: A Report by Her Majesty's Inspectors in Collaboration with the LEAs of Islington, Southwark and Tower Hamlets*. London: Office for Standards in Education.

Peacock, M. and Beard, R. (1997) '"Almost an Invincible Repugnance"? word processors and pupil writers', *Educational Review*, 49, 3, 283–294.

Peters, R.S. (ed.) (1969) *Perspectives on Plowden*. London: Routledge & Kegan Paul.

Phillips, R. and Furlong, J. (eds) (2001) *Education, Reform and the State: Twenty-Five Years of Politics, Policy and Practice*. London: Routledge Falmer.

Raban, B., Clarke, C. and McIntyre, J. (1993) *Evaluation of the Implementation of English in the National Curriculum at Key Stages 1, 2 and 3 (1991–1993): Final Report*. York: National Curriculum Council.

Reinking, D. (1998) 'Introduction: Synthesising Technological Transformations in Literacy in a Post-typographic World' in D. Reinking, M.C. McKenna, L.D. Labbo and R.D. Keiffer (eds) *Handbook of Literacy and Technology* (pp. xi–xxx). Mahwah, NJ: Lawrence Erlbaum.

Reynolds, D. (1998) 'Schooling for Literacy: a review of research on teacher effectiveness and school effectiveness and its implications for contemporary educational policies', *Educational Review*, 50, 2, 147–162.

Reynolds, D., Creemers, B.P.M., Nesselrodt, P.S., Schaffer, E.C., Stringfield, S. and Teddlie, C. (eds) (1994) *Advances in School Effectiveness Research and Practice*. London: Pergamon.

Reynolds, D. and Teddlie, C. (2001) 'Reflections on the Critics, and Beyond Them', *School Effectiveness and School Improvement*, 12, 99–113.

Richards, C. (ed.) (1982) *New Directions in Primary Education*. London: Falmer Press.

Rose, J. (2006) *Independent Review of the Teaching of Early Reading*. London: DfES.

Sainsbury, M., Schagen, I. and Whetton, C. with Hagues, N. and Minnis, M. (1998) *Evaluation of the National Literacy Strategy: Final Report*. Slough: National Foundation for Educational Research.

Scheerens, J. (1992) *Effective Schooling: Research, Theory and Practice*. London: Cassell.

Shorrocks-Taylor, D. (1999) *National Testing: Past, Present and Future*. Leicester: British Psychological Society.

Slavin, R.E. (1997) *Success for All: Policy Implications for British Education*. Paper presented at the Literacy Task Force Conference, London (27 February).

Stannard, J. (1997) *Raising Standards Through the National Literacy Project*. Paper presented at the Literacy Task Force Conference, London (27 February).

Stannard, J. and Huxford, L. (2007) *The Literacy Game*. London: Routledge.

Stanovich, K. (1994) 'Romance and Reality', *The Reading Teacher*, 47, 4, 280–291.

Start, K.B. and Wells, B.K. (1972) *The Trend of Reading Standards*. Slough: National Foundation for Educational Research.

Teddlie, C. and Reynolds, D. (eds) (1999) *The International Handbook of School Effectiveness Research.* Lewes: Falmer Press.

Venezky, R.L. (1970) *The Structure of English Orthography.* The Hague: Mouton.

Waterland, L. (1985) *Read with Me: An Apprenticeship Approach to Reading* (Second edition: 1988). Stroud: Thimble Press.

Watson, J. and Johnson, R. (1998) 'Accelerating Reading Attainment: The effectiveness of synthetic phonics', *Interchange,* 57, Edinburgh: Scottish Office.

Whitehead, F., Capey, A.C. and Maddren, W. (1975) *Children's Reading Interests.* London: Evans/Methuen Educational for the Schools Council.

Whitty, G. (2006) *Teacher Professionalism in a New Era.* Paper presented at the first General Teaching Council for Northern Ireland Annual Lecture, Belfast (March).

Wragg, E.C., Wragg, C.M., Haynes, G.S. and Chamberlain, R.P. (1998) *Improving Literacy in the Primary School.* London: Routledge.